50 Baking with Alternative Flavors Recipes for Home

By: Kelly Johnson

Table of Contents

- Matcha Green Tea Cookies
- Lavender Lemon Cake
- Earl Grey Tea Shortbread
- Chai Spice Muffins
- Chocolate-Coffee Cake
- Sweet Potato Brownies
- Blueberry Basil Scones
- Rosewater Macarons
- Coconut Lime Bars
- Pumpkin Spice Cookies
- Lemon Thyme Pound Cake
- Cinnamon Apple Fritters
- Mint Chocolate Chip Cupcakes
- Honey Almond Biscotti
- Salted Caramel Pretzel Brownies
- Earl Grey Infused Pound Cake
- Zesty Orange Olive Oil Cake
- Ginger Peach Crumble
- Matcha Chiffon Cake
- Lemon Poppy Seed Bread with Honey Glaze
- Pistachio Raspberry Tarts
- Turmeric Banana Bread
- Coconut Pineapple Cake
- Chocolate Dipped Cherry Biscuits
- Choco-Matcha Swirl Brownies
- Bourbon Pecan Pie
- Cardamom Chocolate Chip Cookies
- Mango Coconut Bread
- Coconut Chai Cake
- Rhubarb Ginger Crisp
- Poppy Seed Orange Cookies
- Almond Joy Cupcakes
- Hibiscus Infused Sugar Cookies
- Saffron Rice Pudding Cake
- Raspberry Rose Shortcakes

- Lime Basil Cheesecake
- Carrot Cake with Cream Cheese Ginger Frosting
- Apricot Lavender Muffins
- Lemon Blueberry Ricotta Cake
- Spiced Pear and Ginger Upside Down Cake
- Chocolate Chili Cake
- Vanilla Bean Fig Bread
- Avocado Chocolate Mousse Cake
- Salted Maple Pecan Bars
- Earl Grey Honey Butter Cookies
- Lemon Lavender Popcorn Cookies
- Roasted Beet Red Velvet Cake
- Mocha Hazelnut Cupcakes
- Sweet Corn and Raspberry Muffins
- Bourbon Peach Cobbler

Matcha Green Tea Cookies

Ingredients:

- 1 ½ cups all-purpose flour
- 2 tbsp matcha green tea powder
- ½ cup unsalted butter, softened
- ¾ cup sugar
- 1 large egg
- 1 tsp vanilla extract
- Pinch of salt

Instructions:

1. **Preheat oven** – Set to 350°F (175°C) and line a baking sheet with parchment paper.
2. **Mix dry ingredients** – In a bowl, whisk flour, matcha powder, and salt.
3. **Cream butter and sugar** – Beat softened butter and sugar until light and fluffy, then add egg and vanilla.
4. **Combine** – Gradually add dry ingredients and mix until dough forms.
5. **Shape cookies** – Roll dough into balls, flatten slightly, and place on the baking sheet.
6. **Bake** – Bake for 10–12 minutes, then cool on a wire rack.

Lavender Lemon Cake

Ingredients:

- 1 ½ cups all-purpose flour
- 1 tbsp dried lavender
- 1 tsp baking powder
- 1 tsp lemon zest
- 2 large eggs
- 1 cup sugar
- ½ cup unsalted butter, softened
- ½ cup milk
- 2 tbsp lemon juice

Instructions:

1. **Preheat oven** – Set to 350°F (175°C) and grease a cake pan.
2. **Mix dry ingredients** – Whisk flour, lavender, baking powder, and lemon zest.
3. **Cream butter and sugar** – Beat butter and sugar until fluffy, then add eggs, milk, and lemon juice.
4. **Combine** – Gradually add dry ingredients to the wet mixture, mixing until smooth.
5. **Bake** – Pour batter into the pan and bake for 25–30 minutes.
6. **Serve** – Let cool before slicing and serving.

Earl Grey Tea Shortbread

Ingredients:

- 1 ¾ cups all-purpose flour
- ½ cup unsalted butter, softened
- ¼ cup powdered sugar
- 2 tbsp loose Earl Grey tea (or tea bags)
- 1 tsp vanilla extract
- Pinch of salt

Instructions:

1. **Preheat oven** – Set to 350°F (175°C) and line a baking sheet with parchment paper.
2. **Mix ingredients** – Beat butter and powdered sugar until smooth, then add tea, vanilla, and salt.
3. **Add flour** – Gradually mix in flour until dough forms.
4. **Shape cookies** – Roll dough into a log, chill for 30 minutes, then slice into rounds.
5. **Bake** – Bake for 10–12 minutes, then cool on a wire rack.

Chai Spice Muffins

Ingredients:

- 1 ½ cups all-purpose flour
- 1 tsp ground cinnamon
- ½ tsp ground ginger
- ¼ tsp ground cloves
- 1 tsp baking powder
- ½ tsp baking soda
- 1 cup buttermilk
- ½ cup vegetable oil
- 1 large egg
- ¾ cup brown sugar

Instructions:

1. **Preheat oven** – Set to 350°F (175°C) and line a muffin tin with paper liners.
2. **Mix dry ingredients** – In a bowl, combine flour, spices, baking powder, and baking soda.
3. **Mix wet ingredients** – In another bowl, whisk buttermilk, oil, egg, and brown sugar.
4. **Combine** – Add the wet ingredients to the dry ingredients and mix until just combined.
5. **Bake** – Spoon batter into the muffin tin and bake for 18–20 minutes.

Chocolate-Coffee Cake

Ingredients:

- 1 ½ cups all-purpose flour
- ½ cup cocoa powder
- 1 tsp baking powder
- ½ tsp baking soda
- 1 tsp instant coffee granules
- ½ cup sugar
- ½ cup unsalted butter, softened
- 2 large eggs
- 1 tsp vanilla extract
- ¾ cup sour cream

Instructions:

1. **Preheat oven** – Set to 350°F (175°C) and grease a cake pan.
2. **Mix dry ingredients** – Whisk flour, cocoa powder, baking powder, baking soda, and coffee granules.
3. **Cream butter and sugar** – Beat butter and sugar until fluffy, then add eggs and vanilla.
4. **Add dry ingredients** – Gradually add dry ingredients and sour cream, mixing until smooth.
5. **Bake** – Pour batter into the pan and bake for 30–35 minutes.
6. **Serve** – Let cool and enjoy!

Sweet Potato Brownies

Ingredients:

- 1 cup mashed sweet potato
- 1 cup sugar
- ¾ cup all-purpose flour
- ¼ cup cocoa powder
- 2 large eggs
- ½ tsp vanilla extract
- ¼ tsp salt
- ¼ cup melted coconut oil

Instructions:

1. **Preheat oven** – Set to 350°F (175°C) and grease a baking pan.
2. **Prepare sweet potato** – Mash the sweet potato until smooth.
3. **Mix ingredients** – In a bowl, mix mashed sweet potato, sugar, flour, cocoa powder, eggs, vanilla, salt, and coconut oil.
4. **Bake** – Pour batter into the pan and bake for 20–25 minutes, until a toothpick comes out clean.
5. **Serve** – Let cool before slicing into brownies.

Blueberry Basil Scones

Ingredients:

- 2 cups all-purpose flour
- ½ cup sugar
- 2 tsp baking powder
- 1 tsp fresh basil, finely chopped
- ½ cup cold butter, cubed
- 1 cup fresh blueberries
- 1 egg
- ½ cup milk

Instructions:

1. **Preheat oven** – Set to 375°F (190°C) and line a baking sheet with parchment paper.
2. **Prepare dry ingredients** – Mix flour, sugar, baking powder, and basil.
3. **Cut in butter** – Cut cold butter into the dry mixture until crumbly.
4. **Add wet ingredients** – Stir in blueberries, egg, and milk until combined.
5. **Bake** – Drop spoonfuls of dough onto the baking sheet and bake for 15–18 minutes.

Rosewater Macarons

Ingredients:

- 1 ½ cups powdered sugar
- 1 cup almond flour
- 2 large egg whites
- ¼ cup granulated sugar
- 1 tsp rosewater
- Pink food coloring (optional)

Instructions:

1. **Preheat oven** – Set to 300°F (150°C) and line a baking sheet with parchment paper.
2. **Prepare dry ingredients** – Sift powdered sugar and almond flour together.
3. **Whip egg whites** – Beat egg whites until stiff peaks form, gradually adding granulated sugar.
4. **Fold ingredients** – Gently fold in almond flour mixture, rosewater, and food coloring.
5. **Pipe macarons** – Pipe small circles onto the baking sheet and let them rest for 30 minutes.
6. **Bake** – Bake for 15–18 minutes and cool completely before filling with rosewater buttercream or ganache.

Coconut Lime Bars

Ingredients:

- 1 ½ cups graham cracker crumbs
- ½ cup shredded coconut
- ½ cup melted butter
- 1 cup sweetened condensed milk
- 2 tbsp lime juice
- 1 tbsp lime zest

Instructions:

1. **Preheat oven** – Set to 350°F (175°C) and grease a baking dish.
2. **Prepare crust** – Mix graham cracker crumbs, coconut, and melted butter. Press into the bottom of the dish.
3. **Prepare filling** – In a bowl, mix condensed milk, lime juice, and lime zest. Pour over the crust.
4. **Bake** – Bake for 25–30 minutes until set and lightly golden.
5. **Serve** – Let cool before cutting into squares. Enjoy!

Pumpkin Spice Cookies

Ingredients:

- 1 ½ cups all-purpose flour
- 1 tsp baking soda
- 1 tsp ground cinnamon
- ½ tsp ground ginger
- ¼ tsp ground cloves
- ½ tsp salt
- ½ cup unsalted butter, softened
- 1 cup pumpkin puree
- 1 cup brown sugar
- 1 large egg
- 1 tsp vanilla extract

Instructions:

1. **Preheat oven** – Set to 350°F (175°C) and line a baking sheet with parchment paper.
2. **Mix dry ingredients** – In a bowl, whisk together flour, baking soda, cinnamon, ginger, cloves, and salt.
3. **Prepare wet ingredients** – In another bowl, beat butter, pumpkin puree, brown sugar, egg, and vanilla until smooth.
4. **Combine** – Gradually add dry ingredients to the wet mixture and mix until just combined.
5. **Shape cookies** – Drop spoonfuls of dough onto the baking sheet.
6. **Bake** – Bake for 10–12 minutes, then let cool.

Lemon Thyme Pound Cake

Ingredients:

- 1 ½ cups all-purpose flour
- 1 tsp baking powder
- ½ tsp salt
- 1 stick unsalted butter, softened
- 1 cup sugar
- 2 large eggs
- 1 tsp vanilla extract
- Zest of 1 lemon
- 1 tbsp fresh thyme leaves
- ½ cup milk

Instructions:

1. **Preheat oven** – Set to 350°F (175°C) and grease a loaf pan.
2. **Mix dry ingredients** – In a bowl, whisk flour, baking powder, and salt.
3. **Cream butter and sugar** – Beat butter and sugar until fluffy, then add eggs, vanilla, lemon zest, and thyme.
4. **Add flour mixture** – Gradually mix in the dry ingredients, alternating with milk.
5. **Bake** – Pour into the loaf pan and bake for 55–60 minutes.
6. **Serve** – Let cool before slicing.

Cinnamon Apple Fritters

Ingredients:

- 1 cup all-purpose flour
- 1 tsp baking powder
- 1 tsp cinnamon
- ¼ tsp salt
- 1 large egg
- 1/3 cup milk
- 2 medium apples, peeled and chopped
- 2 tbsp sugar
- Oil for frying

Instructions:

1. **Prepare batter** – In a bowl, mix flour, baking powder, cinnamon, and salt. Add egg and milk, stirring to combine.
2. **Add apples** – Fold in chopped apples and sugar.
3. **Fry fritters** – Heat oil in a pan, then spoon batter into the oil and fry until golden on both sides.
4. **Serve** – Drain on paper towels and dust with powdered sugar.

Mint Chocolate Chip Cupcakes

Ingredients:

- 1 ½ cups all-purpose flour
- 1 tsp baking powder
- ½ tsp salt
- ½ cup unsalted butter, softened
- 1 cup sugar
- 2 large eggs
- 1 tsp vanilla extract
- ¼ tsp mint extract
- ½ cup milk
- ½ cup mini chocolate chips

Instructions:

1. **Preheat oven** – Set to 350°F (175°C) and line a cupcake tin with paper liners.
2. **Mix dry ingredients** – In a bowl, whisk flour, baking powder, and salt.
3. **Cream butter and sugar** – Beat butter and sugar until fluffy, then add eggs, vanilla, and mint extract.
4. **Add dry ingredients** – Gradually add dry ingredients, alternating with milk, until combined.
5. **Add chocolate chips** – Gently fold in mini chocolate chips.
6. **Bake** – Spoon batter into cupcake liners and bake for 18–20 minutes.

Honey Almond Biscotti

Ingredients:

- 1 ¾ cups all-purpose flour
- ½ tsp baking powder
- ¼ tsp salt
- 2 large eggs
- 1 cup sugar
- 2 tbsp honey
- 1 tsp vanilla extract
- 1 cup sliced almonds

Instructions:

1. **Preheat oven** – Set to 350°F (175°C) and line a baking sheet with parchment paper.
2. **Mix dry ingredients** – In a bowl, whisk flour, baking powder, and salt.
3. **Prepare wet ingredients** – In another bowl, beat eggs, sugar, honey, and vanilla until smooth.
4. **Combine** – Gradually add dry ingredients, then fold in almonds.
5. **Shape dough** – Shape dough into a log and bake for 25 minutes.
6. **Slice and bake again** – Slice the log into pieces and bake for an additional 10–12 minutes.

Salted Caramel Pretzel Brownies

Ingredients:

- 1 box brownie mix
- 1 cup mini pretzels
- ½ cup salted caramel sauce
- ½ cup chocolate chips

Instructions:

1. **Preheat oven** – Set to 350°F (175°C) and grease a baking pan.
2. **Prepare brownies** – Make brownies according to package instructions.
3. **Add pretzels** – Sprinkle mini pretzels on top of the brownie batter before baking.
4. **Bake** – Bake as directed, then drizzle with salted caramel sauce and chocolate chips.
5. **Serve** – Let cool before cutting into squares.

Earl Grey Infused Pound Cake

Ingredients:

- 1 ½ cups all-purpose flour
- 1 tsp baking powder
- ¼ tsp salt
- 1 stick unsalted butter, softened
- 1 cup sugar
- 2 large eggs
- 1 tsp vanilla extract
- 2 tbsp Earl Grey tea leaves, finely ground
- ½ cup milk

Instructions:

1. **Preheat oven** – Set to 350°F (175°C) and grease a loaf pan.
2. **Mix dry ingredients** – In a bowl, whisk flour, baking powder, salt, and Earl Grey tea.
3. **Cream butter and sugar** – Beat butter and sugar until fluffy, then add eggs and vanilla.
4. **Add dry ingredients** – Gradually add the dry ingredients, alternating with milk.
5. **Bake** – Pour into the loaf pan and bake for 45–50 minutes.

Zesty Orange Olive Oil Cake

Ingredients:

- 1 ½ cups all-purpose flour
- 1 tsp baking powder
- ¼ tsp salt
- 1 cup sugar
- 3 large eggs
- 1 cup olive oil
- Zest of 2 oranges
- ½ cup orange juice

Instructions:

1. **Preheat oven** – Set to 350°F (175°C) and grease a cake pan.
2. **Mix dry ingredients** – In a bowl, whisk flour, baking powder, and salt.
3. **Prepare wet ingredients** – In another bowl, whisk eggs, sugar, olive oil, orange zest, and juice.
4. **Combine** – Gradually add dry ingredients to the wet mixture.
5. **Bake** – Pour batter into the pan and bake for 35–40 minutes.

Ginger Peach Crumble

Ingredients:

- 4 ripe peaches, peeled and sliced
- 1 tsp ground ginger
- 1 tbsp sugar
- 1 cup rolled oats
- ½ cup all-purpose flour
- 1/3 cup brown sugar
- ¼ cup cold butter, cubed

Instructions:

1. **Preheat oven** – Set to 350°F (175°C) and grease a baking dish.
2. **Prepare peaches** – Toss sliced peaches with ginger and sugar, then spread in the baking dish.
3. **Prepare crumble topping** – Mix oats, flour, brown sugar, and cold butter until crumbly.
4. **Assemble and bake** – Spread the crumble mixture over the peaches and bake for 30–35 minutes until golden.

Matcha Chiffon Cake

Ingredients:

- 1 ½ cups all-purpose flour
- 1 tsp matcha green tea powder
- 1 tsp baking powder
- ¼ tsp salt
- 6 large eggs, separated
- 1 cup sugar
- ¼ cup vegetable oil
- ½ tsp vanilla extract
- ¼ cup warm water

Instructions:

1. **Preheat oven** – Set to 325°F (165°C) and grease a chiffon cake pan.
2. **Mix dry ingredients** – In a bowl, whisk flour, matcha powder, baking powder, and salt.
3. **Beat egg whites** – In a separate bowl, beat egg whites until stiff peaks form.
4. **Mix wet ingredients** – In another bowl, whisk egg yolks, sugar, oil, vanilla, and warm water.
5. **Combine** – Gradually fold dry ingredients into the wet mixture, then gently fold in egg whites.
6. **Bake** – Pour batter into the pan and bake for 45–50 minutes.

Lemon Poppy Seed Bread with Honey Glaze

Ingredients:

- 1 ½ cups all-purpose flour
- 1 tsp baking powder
- ½ tsp baking soda
- ¼ tsp salt
- 2 tbsp poppy seeds
- 1 cup sugar
- 2 large eggs
- ½ cup vegetable oil
- 1 cup buttermilk
- 2 tbsp lemon juice
- Zest of 1 lemon
- ¼ cup honey (for glaze)

Instructions:

1. **Preheat oven** – Set to 350°F (175°C) and grease a loaf pan.
2. **Mix dry ingredients** – In a bowl, whisk flour, baking powder, baking soda, salt, and poppy seeds.
3. **Prepare wet ingredients** – In another bowl, beat eggs with sugar, oil, buttermilk, lemon juice, and zest.
4. **Combine** – Gradually add dry ingredients to the wet mixture and stir until smooth.
5. **Bake** – Pour batter into the loaf pan and bake for 50–55 minutes.
6. **Prepare glaze** – Warm honey and drizzle over the cooled bread.

Pistachio Raspberry Tarts

Ingredients:

- 1 cup shelled pistachios
- ¾ cup all-purpose flour
- 2 tbsp powdered sugar
- ½ cup unsalted butter, cold
- 1 large egg yolk
- 1 tsp vanilla extract
- ¼ cup raspberry jam
- Fresh raspberries for garnish

Instructions:

1. **Preheat oven** – Set to 350°F (175°C) and grease tart pans.
2. **Prepare crust** – In a food processor, blend pistachios, flour, powdered sugar, and butter until crumbly. Add egg yolk and vanilla, then pulse until dough forms.
3. **Shape crust** – Press dough into tart pans and bake for 10–12 minutes, until lightly golden.
4. **Fill with jam** – Once cooled, fill with raspberry jam and garnish with fresh raspberries.

Turmeric Banana Bread

Ingredients:

- 1 ½ cups all-purpose flour
- 1 tsp turmeric powder
- 1 tsp baking soda
- ½ tsp salt
- 3 ripe bananas, mashed
- ½ cup sugar
- 2 large eggs
- ¼ cup melted butter
- 1 tsp vanilla extract
- ¼ cup buttermilk

Instructions:

1. **Preheat oven** – Set to 350°F (175°C) and grease a loaf pan.
2. **Mix dry ingredients** – In a bowl, whisk flour, turmeric, baking soda, and salt.
3. **Prepare wet ingredients** – In another bowl, combine mashed bananas, sugar, eggs, melted butter, vanilla, and buttermilk.
4. **Combine** – Stir dry ingredients into the wet mixture and pour into the loaf pan.
5. **Bake** – Bake for 50–55 minutes until golden and a toothpick comes out clean.

Coconut Pineapple Cake

Ingredients:

- 1 ½ cups all-purpose flour
- 1 tsp baking powder
- 1 tsp baking soda
- ½ tsp salt
- 1 cup shredded coconut
- 1 cup crushed pineapple, drained
- 1 cup sugar
- 2 large eggs
- ½ cup vegetable oil
- 1 tsp vanilla extract
- ¼ cup coconut milk

Instructions:

1. **Preheat oven** – Set to 350°F (175°C) and grease a cake pan.
2. **Mix dry ingredients** – In a bowl, whisk flour, baking powder, baking soda, salt, and shredded coconut.
3. **Combine wet ingredients** – In another bowl, mix pineapple, sugar, eggs, oil, vanilla, and coconut milk.
4. **Combine** – Gradually fold the wet mixture into the dry ingredients until smooth.
5. **Bake** – Pour batter into the cake pan and bake for 30–35 minutes.

Chocolate Dipped Cherry Biscuits

Ingredients:

- 2 cups all-purpose flour
- 1 tbsp baking powder
- ¼ tsp salt
- ½ cup unsalted butter, cold and cubed
- ¾ cup heavy cream
- 1 cup maraschino cherries, drained and chopped
- ½ cup semisweet chocolate chips

Instructions:

1. **Preheat oven** – Set to 375°F (190°C) and line a baking sheet with parchment paper.
2. **Prepare dough** – In a bowl, whisk flour, baking powder, and salt. Cut in the butter until the mixture resembles coarse crumbs.
3. **Add cream and cherries** – Stir in heavy cream and chopped cherries until dough forms.
4. **Shape biscuits** – Drop spoonfuls of dough onto the baking sheet and bake for 12–15 minutes.
5. **Dip in chocolate** – Melt chocolate chips and dip the tops of the biscuits into the chocolate. Let cool.

Choco-Matcha Swirl Brownies

Ingredients:

- 1 cup unsalted butter
- 1 cup sugar
- 3 large eggs
- 1 tsp vanilla extract
- 1 cup all-purpose flour
- ½ cup cocoa powder
- 2 tbsp matcha powder
- ½ tsp baking powder
- ¼ tsp salt

Instructions:

1. **Preheat oven** – Set to 350°F (175°C) and grease a baking pan.
2. **Prepare brownie base** – In a bowl, melt butter and mix with sugar, eggs, and vanilla. Stir in flour, cocoa powder, baking powder, and salt.
3. **Make matcha swirl** – Mix matcha powder with a little water to form a paste, then fold into part of the brownie batter.
4. **Layer and swirl** – Spoon the matcha batter over the chocolate batter in the pan and swirl with a knife.
5. **Bake** – Bake for 25–30 minutes until set.

Bourbon Pecan Pie

Ingredients:

- 1 pre-made pie crust
- 1 ½ cups pecan halves
- ¾ cup dark corn syrup
- ½ cup brown sugar
- 3 large eggs
- 2 tbsp bourbon
- 1 tsp vanilla extract
- ¼ tsp salt

Instructions:

1. **Preheat oven** – Set to 350°F (175°C).
2. **Prepare filling** – In a bowl, whisk corn syrup, brown sugar, eggs, bourbon, vanilla, and salt.
3. **Assemble pie** – Spread pecans in the pie crust and pour the filling over the top.
4. **Bake** – Bake for 45–50 minutes until the filling is set.
5. **Serve** – Let cool before serving.

Cardamom Chocolate Chip Cookies

Ingredients:

- 2 ¼ cups all-purpose flour
- 1 tsp ground cardamom
- 1 tsp baking soda
- ½ tsp salt
- 1 cup unsalted butter, softened
- 1 cup brown sugar
- 1 large egg
- 1 tsp vanilla extract
- 1 ½ cups chocolate chips

Instructions:

1. **Preheat oven** – Set to 350°F (175°C) and line a baking sheet with parchment paper.
2. **Mix dry ingredients** – In a bowl, whisk flour, cardamom, baking soda, and salt.
3. **Cream butter and sugar** – Beat butter and brown sugar until light and fluffy, then add egg and vanilla.
4. **Combine** – Gradually add dry ingredients and fold in chocolate chips.
5. **Bake** – Drop spoonfuls of dough onto the baking sheet and bake for 10–12 minutes.

Mango Coconut Bread

Ingredients:

- 1 ½ cups all-purpose flour
- 1 tsp baking powder
- ½ tsp baking soda
- ¼ tsp salt
- 1 cup coconut milk
- 1 cup mashed ripe mango
- 1/3 cup shredded coconut
- 1/2 cup sugar
- 1 large egg

Instructions:

1. **Preheat oven** – Set to 350°F (175°C) and grease a loaf pan.
2. **Mix dry ingredients** – In a bowl, whisk flour, baking powder, baking soda, and salt.
3. **Combine wet ingredients** – In another bowl, mix coconut milk, mango, shredded coconut, sugar, and egg.
4. **Combine** – Gradually add dry ingredients to the wet mixture.
5. **Bake** – Pour batter into the pan and bake for 45–50 minutes.

Coconut Chai Cake

Ingredients:

- 1 ½ cups all-purpose flour
- 1 tsp baking powder
- 1 tsp chai spice mix (cinnamon, cardamom, ginger, cloves)
- ½ tsp salt
- 1 cup shredded coconut
- 1 cup sugar
- ½ cup unsalted butter, softened
- 2 large eggs
- 1 tsp vanilla extract
- 1 cup coconut milk

Instructions:

1. **Preheat oven** – Set to 350°F (175°C) and grease a cake pan.
2. **Mix dry ingredients** – In a bowl, whisk flour, baking powder, chai spices, salt, and coconut.
3. **Cream butter and sugar** – Beat butter and sugar until fluffy, then add eggs and vanilla.
4. **Combine** – Gradually add the dry ingredients and coconut milk, mixing until smooth.
5. **Bake** – Pour batter into the pan and bake for 30–35 minutes.
6. **Serve** – Let cool before slicing and serving.

Rhubarb Ginger Crisp

Ingredients:

- 4 cups rhubarb, chopped
- 1 tsp grated fresh ginger
- ¾ cup sugar
- 1 tbsp cornstarch
- 1 ½ cups rolled oats
- ½ cup flour
- ¼ cup brown sugar
- 1 tsp cinnamon
- ¼ tsp salt
- ½ cup unsalted butter, melted

Instructions:

1. **Preheat oven** – Set to 375°F (190°C) and grease a baking dish.
2. **Prepare rhubarb filling** – Toss rhubarb with ginger, sugar, cornstarch, and a pinch of cinnamon. Place in the prepared dish.
3. **Prepare topping** – In a separate bowl, mix oats, flour, brown sugar, cinnamon, salt, and melted butter.
4. **Assemble** – Sprinkle topping over rhubarb mixture.
5. **Bake** – Bake for 40–45 minutes until the topping is golden and the filling is bubbling.

Poppy Seed Orange Cookies

Ingredients:

- 1 ½ cups all-purpose flour
- 2 tbsp poppy seeds
- 1 tsp baking powder
- ½ tsp salt
- ½ cup unsalted butter, softened
- 1 cup sugar
- 1 large egg
- Zest of 1 orange
- 2 tbsp fresh orange juice

Instructions:

1. **Preheat oven** – Set to 350°F (175°C) and line a baking sheet with parchment paper.
2. **Mix dry ingredients** – In a bowl, whisk flour, poppy seeds, baking powder, and salt.
3. **Cream butter and sugar** – Beat butter and sugar until fluffy, then add egg, orange zest, and orange juice.
4. **Combine** – Gradually add dry ingredients and mix until smooth.
5. **Shape cookies** – Roll dough into balls and place on the baking sheet. Flatten slightly.
6. **Bake** – Bake for 10–12 minutes until golden.

Almond Joy Cupcakes

Ingredients:

- 1 ½ cups all-purpose flour
- 1 tsp baking powder
- ½ tsp salt
- ½ cup unsalted butter, softened
- 1 cup sugar
- 2 large eggs
- 1 tsp vanilla extract
- ½ cup milk
- ½ cup shredded coconut
- ¼ cup chopped almonds
- ¼ cup chocolate chips

Instructions:

1. **Preheat oven** – Set to 350°F (175°C) and line a muffin tin with paper liners.
2. **Mix dry ingredients** – In a bowl, whisk flour, baking powder, and salt.
3. **Prepare wet ingredients** – In another bowl, beat butter and sugar until fluffy, then add eggs and vanilla.
4. **Combine** – Gradually add dry ingredients and milk, mixing until smooth.
5. **Add mix-ins** – Stir in coconut, almonds, and chocolate chips.
6. **Bake** – Pour batter into the muffin tin and bake for 18–20 minutes.

Hibiscus Infused Sugar Cookies

Ingredients:

- 2 ½ cups all-purpose flour
- 1 tsp baking powder
- ¼ tsp salt
- 1 cup unsalted butter, softened
- 1 ¼ cups sugar
- 1 large egg
- 2 tbsp dried hibiscus flowers, ground
- 1 tsp vanilla extract

Instructions:

1. **Preheat oven** – Set to 350°F (175°C) and line a baking sheet with parchment paper.
2. **Mix dry ingredients** – In a bowl, whisk flour, baking powder, salt, and ground hibiscus.
3. **Cream butter and sugar** – Beat butter and sugar until fluffy, then add egg and vanilla.
4. **Combine** – Gradually add dry ingredients and mix until smooth.
5. **Shape cookies** – Roll dough into balls and flatten slightly on the baking sheet.
6. **Bake** – Bake for 10–12 minutes until golden.

Saffron Rice Pudding Cake

Ingredients:

- 1 ½ cups cooked rice
- 1 cup whole milk
- ½ cup sugar
- 2 large eggs
- ½ tsp vanilla extract
- Pinch of saffron threads
- ¼ tsp ground cardamom

Instructions:

1. **Preheat oven** – Set to 350°F (175°C) and grease a baking dish.
2. **Prepare saffron milk** – Soak saffron threads in warm milk for 10 minutes.
3. **Mix ingredients** – In a bowl, whisk eggs, sugar, vanilla, and cardamom. Add the saffron-infused milk and cooked rice, mixing until combined.
4. **Bake** – Pour mixture into the baking dish and bake for 40–45 minutes until set.
5. **Serve** – Let cool before slicing and serving.

Raspberry Rose Shortcakes

Ingredients:

- 1 ½ cups all-purpose flour
- 2 tbsp sugar
- 1 tbsp baking powder
- ½ tsp salt
- 1 stick unsalted butter, cold and cubed
- ½ cup milk
- 1 cup fresh raspberries
- 1 tbsp rosewater
- Whipped cream for serving

Instructions:

1. **Preheat oven** – Set to 375°F (190°C) and line a baking sheet with parchment paper.
2. **Prepare shortcakes** – In a bowl, mix flour, sugar, baking powder, and salt. Cut in butter until the mixture resembles coarse crumbs. Add milk and stir until dough forms.
3. **Shape and bake** – Drop spoonfuls of dough onto the baking sheet and bake for 12–15 minutes.
4. **Prepare raspberries** – Mix raspberries with rosewater and set aside.
5. **Assemble** – Slice shortcakes in half, top with raspberries, and serve with whipped cream.

Lime Basil Cheesecake

Ingredients:

- 1 ½ cups graham cracker crumbs
- ¼ cup sugar
- ¼ cup unsalted butter, melted
- 3 (8 oz) cream cheese blocks, softened
- 1 cup sugar
- 2 large eggs
- 1 tsp vanilla extract
- Zest and juice of 2 limes
- ¼ cup fresh basil, finely chopped

Instructions:

1. **Preheat oven** – Set to 325°F (160°C) and grease a springform pan.
2. **Prepare crust** – Mix graham cracker crumbs, sugar, and melted butter. Press into the bottom of the pan.
3. **Make filling** – Beat cream cheese and sugar until smooth. Add eggs, vanilla, lime zest, and juice, then stir in basil.
4. **Assemble and bake** – Pour filling into the crust and bake for 50–60 minutes.
5. **Serve** – Let cool, refrigerate for 4 hours, and serve chilled.

Carrot Cake with Cream Cheese Ginger Frosting

Ingredients:

- 1 ½ cups all-purpose flour
- 1 tsp baking powder
- 1 tsp baking soda
- 1 tsp ground cinnamon
- ½ tsp ground ginger
- ¼ tsp salt
- 2 cups grated carrots
- 1 cup sugar
- 2 large eggs
- ½ cup vegetable oil
- 1 tsp vanilla extract

For frosting:

- 8 oz cream cheese, softened
- ½ cup unsalted butter, softened
- 2 cups powdered sugar
- 1 tsp ground ginger

Instructions:

1. **Preheat oven** – Set to 350°F (175°C) and grease a cake pan.
2. **Mix dry ingredients** – In a bowl, whisk flour, baking powder, baking soda, cinnamon, ginger, and salt.
3. **Prepare wet ingredients** – In another bowl, mix grated carrots, sugar, eggs, oil, and vanilla.
4. **Combine** – Gradually add dry ingredients to the wet mixture and pour into the pan.
5. **Bake** – Bake for 35–40 minutes until a toothpick comes out clean.
6. **Make frosting** – Beat cream cheese, butter, powdered sugar, and ginger until smooth.
7. **Frost and serve** – Let cake cool, frost with ginger cream cheese frosting, and serve.

Apricot Lavender Muffins

Ingredients:

- 1 ½ cups all-purpose flour
- 1 tsp baking powder
- ½ tsp baking soda
- ¼ tsp salt
- ½ tsp dried lavender buds
- 1 cup dried apricots, chopped
- 1 cup sugar
- 2 large eggs
- ½ cup unsalted butter, melted
- 1 cup buttermilk
- 1 tsp vanilla extract

Instructions:

1. **Preheat oven** – Set to 350°F (175°C) and line a muffin tin with paper liners.
2. **Mix dry ingredients** – In a bowl, whisk flour, baking powder, baking soda, salt, and lavender.
3. **Prepare wet ingredients** – In another bowl, beat sugar, eggs, melted butter, buttermilk, and vanilla.
4. **Combine** – Gradually add dry ingredients to wet, then fold in chopped apricots.
5. **Bake** – Spoon batter into muffin cups and bake for 18–20 minutes.

Lemon Blueberry Ricotta Cake

Ingredients:

- 1 ½ cups all-purpose flour
- 1 tsp baking powder
- ½ tsp salt
- 1 cup ricotta cheese
- ½ cup sugar
- 2 large eggs
- 2 tbsp lemon juice
- Zest of 1 lemon
- 1 tsp vanilla extract
- 1 cup fresh blueberries

Instructions:

1. **Preheat oven** – Set to 350°F (175°C) and grease a cake pan.
2. **Mix dry ingredients** – In a bowl, whisk flour, baking powder, and salt.
3. **Prepare wet ingredients** – In another bowl, mix ricotta, sugar, eggs, lemon juice, lemon zest, and vanilla.
4. **Combine** – Gradually add dry ingredients to wet, then gently fold in blueberries.
5. **Bake** – Pour batter into the pan and bake for 35–40 minutes, until golden.

Spiced Pear and Ginger Upside Down Cake

Ingredients:

- 2 ripe pears, peeled and sliced
- 1 tbsp ground ginger
- 1 tsp cinnamon
- ¼ cup brown sugar
- 1 cup all-purpose flour
- 1 tsp baking powder
- ½ tsp baking soda
- ¼ tsp salt
- ½ cup unsalted butter, softened
- 1 cup sugar
- 2 large eggs
- ½ cup milk
- 1 tsp vanilla extract

Instructions:

1. **Preheat oven** – Set to 350°F (175°C) and grease a cake pan.
2. **Prepare pear topping** – In the pan, combine brown sugar, cinnamon, and ground ginger. Arrange pear slices on top.
3. **Make batter** – In a bowl, mix flour, baking powder, baking soda, and salt. In another bowl, cream butter and sugar, then add eggs, milk, and vanilla.
4. **Combine** – Gradually add dry ingredients to wet mixture.
5. **Assemble and bake** – Pour batter over pears and bake for 30–35 minutes. Flip onto a serving plate once cooled.

Chocolate Chili Cake

Ingredients:

- 1 ½ cups all-purpose flour
- 1 tsp baking powder
- ½ tsp baking soda
- 1 tsp ground cinnamon
- ¼ tsp cayenne pepper (adjust for spice preference)
- 1 cup sugar
- ½ cup unsalted butter, softened
- 2 large eggs
- 1 cup cocoa powder
- 1 cup buttermilk
- 1 tsp vanilla extract

Instructions:

1. **Preheat oven** – Set to 350°F (175°C) and grease a cake pan.
2. **Mix dry ingredients** – In a bowl, whisk flour, baking powder, baking soda, cinnamon, and cayenne pepper.
3. **Prepare wet ingredients** – In another bowl, beat butter and sugar until fluffy, then add eggs and vanilla.
4. **Combine** – Add cocoa powder and dry ingredients alternately with buttermilk, mixing until smooth.
5. **Bake** – Pour batter into the pan and bake for 30–35 minutes.

Vanilla Bean Fig Bread

Ingredients:

- 1 ½ cups all-purpose flour
- 1 tsp baking soda
- ½ tsp salt
- 1 tsp vanilla bean paste
- 1 cup chopped dried figs
- ¾ cup sugar
- 1 large egg
- ½ cup unsalted butter, melted
- ½ cup milk

Instructions:

1. **Preheat oven** – Set to 350°F (175°C) and grease a loaf pan.
2. **Mix dry ingredients** – In a bowl, whisk flour, baking soda, and salt.
3. **Prepare wet ingredients** – In another bowl, mix vanilla bean paste, sugar, egg, melted butter, and milk.
4. **Combine** – Gradually add dry ingredients and fold in chopped figs.
5. **Bake** – Pour batter into the loaf pan and bake for 50–55 minutes.

Avocado Chocolate Mousse Cake

Ingredients:

- 2 ripe avocados, peeled and pitted
- 1 cup unsweetened cocoa powder
- 1 cup sugar
- 2 large eggs
- 1 tsp vanilla extract
- ¼ cup melted dark chocolate
- ½ cup coconut oil, melted

Instructions:

1. **Preheat oven** – Set to 350°F (175°C) and grease a cake pan.
2. **Blend ingredients** – In a blender, combine avocado, cocoa powder, sugar, eggs, vanilla, melted chocolate, and coconut oil. Blend until smooth.
3. **Bake** – Pour the mixture into the pan and bake for 20–25 minutes, until set.
4. **Serve** – Let cool before serving for a creamy, rich dessert.

Salted Maple Pecan Bars

Ingredients:

- 1 ½ cups all-purpose flour
- 1 cup chopped pecans
- ½ cup unsalted butter, softened
- ¼ cup brown sugar
- 1 egg
- ½ cup maple syrup
- ½ tsp salt

Instructions:

1. **Preheat oven** – Set to 350°F (175°C) and grease a baking pan.
2. **Prepare dough** – Mix flour, pecans, butter, and brown sugar until crumbly. Press into the bottom of the pan and bake for 12–15 minutes.
3. **Make filling** – In a bowl, whisk egg, maple syrup, and salt. Pour over the crust and bake for another 15–18 minutes until set.
4. **Cool and serve** – Let cool completely before slicing into bars.

Earl Grey Honey Butter Cookies

Ingredients:

- 2 ½ cups all-purpose flour
- 1 tsp baking powder
- 1 tbsp Earl Grey tea leaves
- ½ tsp salt
- 1 cup unsalted butter, softened
- ½ cup honey
- 1 tsp vanilla extract

Instructions:

1. **Preheat oven** – Set to 350°F (175°C) and line a baking sheet with parchment paper.
2. **Mix dry ingredients** – In a bowl, whisk flour, baking powder, tea leaves, and salt.
3. **Cream butter and honey** – Beat butter and honey until fluffy, then add vanilla.
4. **Combine** – Gradually add dry ingredients and mix until smooth.
5. **Shape and bake** – Roll dough into balls, flatten slightly, and bake for 10–12 minutes.

Lemon Lavender Popcorn Cookies

Ingredients:

- 2 cups all-purpose flour
- ½ tsp baking powder
- ¼ tsp salt
- 1 tbsp dried lavender buds
- Zest of 1 lemon
- 1 cup popcorn, popped
- 1 cup unsalted butter, softened
- ¾ cup sugar
- 1 large egg

Instructions:

1. **Preheat oven** – Set to 350°F (175°C) and line a baking sheet with parchment paper.
2. **Mix dry ingredients** – In a bowl, whisk flour, baking powder, salt, lavender, and lemon zest.
3. **Cream butter and sugar** – Beat butter and sugar until fluffy, then add egg and mix until combined.
4. **Combine** – Gradually add dry ingredients and fold in popcorn.
5. **Shape and bake** – Drop spoonfuls of dough onto the sheet and bake for 10–12 minutes.

Roasted Beet Red Velvet Cake

Ingredients:

- 2 cups all-purpose flour
- 1 tsp baking powder
- 1 tsp baking soda
- ½ tsp salt
- 1 cup roasted beet puree
- 1 cup sugar
- 2 large eggs
- ½ cup vegetable oil
- 1 tsp vanilla extract
- 1 tsp cocoa powder

Instructions:

1. **Preheat oven** – Set to 350°F (175°C) and grease a cake pan.
2. **Mix dry ingredients** – In a bowl, whisk flour, baking powder, baking soda, salt, and cocoa powder.
3. **Prepare beet mixture** – In another bowl, whisk beet puree, sugar, eggs, oil, and vanilla.
4. **Combine** – Gradually add dry ingredients to the wet mixture and stir until smooth.
5. **Bake** – Pour batter into the pan and bake for 25–30 minutes, or until a toothpick comes out clean.

Mocha Hazelnut Cupcakes

Ingredients:

- 1 ½ cups all-purpose flour
- 1 tsp baking powder
- ½ tsp baking soda
- ¼ tsp salt
- ½ cup unsweetened cocoa powder
- 1 tbsp instant coffee granules
- 1 cup sugar
- 2 large eggs
- ½ cup vegetable oil
- 1 tsp vanilla extract
- ½ cup buttermilk
- ½ cup chopped hazelnuts

Instructions:

1. **Preheat oven** – Set to 350°F (175°C) and line a muffin tin with paper liners.
2. **Mix dry ingredients** – In a bowl, whisk flour, baking powder, baking soda, salt, cocoa powder, and coffee granules.
3. **Prepare wet ingredients** – In another bowl, mix sugar, eggs, oil, vanilla, and buttermilk until smooth.
4. **Combine** – Gradually add dry ingredients to the wet mixture, mixing until smooth.
5. **Bake** – Spoon batter into muffin liners and sprinkle with hazelnuts. Bake for 18–20 minutes.

Sweet Corn and Raspberry Muffins

Ingredients:

- 1 cup cornmeal
- 1 cup all-purpose flour
- 1 tbsp baking powder
- ½ tsp salt
- 1 cup sugar
- 2 large eggs
- ½ cup milk
- ¼ cup vegetable oil
- 1 cup fresh raspberries

Instructions:

1. **Preheat oven** – Set to 375°F (190°C) and line a muffin tin with paper liners.
2. **Mix dry ingredients** – In a bowl, whisk cornmeal, flour, baking powder, salt, and sugar.
3. **Prepare wet ingredients** – In another bowl, beat eggs, milk, and oil until smooth.
4. **Combine** – Gradually add dry ingredients to the wet mixture and gently fold in raspberries.
5. **Bake** – Spoon batter into muffin cups and bake for 18–20 minutes.

Bourbon Peach Cobbler

Ingredients:

- 4 cups fresh peaches, sliced
- 1 tbsp bourbon
- 1 tbsp lemon juice
- ¼ cup sugar
- 1 ½ cups all-purpose flour
- 1 tsp baking powder
- ½ tsp salt
- ¾ cup milk
- ¼ cup unsalted butter, melted
- ¼ cup brown sugar

Instructions:

1. **Preheat oven** – Set to 375°F (190°C) and grease a baking dish.
2. **Prepare peaches** – Toss sliced peaches with bourbon, lemon juice, and sugar, then place in the baking dish.
3. **Make batter** – In a bowl, whisk flour, baking powder, and salt. Add milk, melted butter, and brown sugar, mixing until smooth.
4. **Assemble** – Pour the batter over the peaches.
5. **Bake** – Bake for 35–40 minutes, until golden and bubbling.

www.ingramcontent.com/pod-product-compliance
Lightning Source LLC
LaVergne TN
LVHW061953070526
838199LV00060B/4093